Unlimited You

Overcoming Obstacles in Life

You can live a JOY-Filled Life

UNLIMITED YOU
Overcoming Obstacles in Life

Grace Empowered Living
(720) 279-4134

www.GraceEmpoweredLiving.com

Printed in the United States of America.

Copyright © 2014 by Grace Empowered Publications

ISBN 978-1500564148

Dedication

We dedicate this book first to those have had a deep yearning to win in life but have been stifled for one reason or another. Your pursuit to no longer be held back inspires all of us to dream and make a difference in our world. May this book provide a pathway to explore what indeed is possible for your life.

To Bern Moses who inspired parts of this book. Your pursuit to be a positive contributive voice continues on long after you have been gone.

"Opportunity often comes disguised in the form of misfortune, or temporary defeat."

~ Napoleon Hill

TABLE OF CONTENTS

Our outside world view contains and restricts us because it is based upon the beliefs of our experiences and perceptions, which are very subjective.

~Scott Johnson – Empowered

Introduction

Has stress and anxiety stopped you from getting what it is you want out of life? Have there been obstacles, events from your past or present that have suffocated your dream?

There are two great events you will experience in life.

1. The day you were born
2. The day you find out why you were born

Discovering both is cause for celebration! Realizing the thing you were born for is exhilarating. Sadly, there are many things that can get in the way of you experiencing the second. You start out in one direction and end up somewhere you never thought possible.

What is the secret to thriving in life when it seems that everything is going against you? That is what this book is about; discovering how to move past the challenges, obstacles, frustrations and fears of life.

The second part is meant to assist and inspire you in making some positive steps toward what it is you want out of life. Ask most people how to make this happen and they will tell you that it would be an easier task to climb Mt. Everest or swim across the great Atlantic Ocean. The fact is that all of us have enough troubles to last a lifetime. Get past one problem and there seems to always be another one ready to show up.

I don't know about you, but I like quick and easy! I love being able to heat things up quickly using my microwave oven, I want to be able to go through the drive-through and order all my problems gone and two orders of tranquility!

If I could wave a magic wand and make my problems go away, I would be the first person to sign up. Oh and by the way, I would have titled this book differently as well. How about, *The One Step Miracle Method For Making All Your Problems Disappear Instantly!* Hey, that sounds pretty good doesn't it? The problem is, it has nothing to do with reality.

If it were this easy I would just have two pages to this book. Page one would ask you to simply answer the following question.

Step 1: All my problems started when _____ (fill in the blank) came into my life.

Step 2: Page two would instruct you to get rid of whatever you're your answer was in step 1.

Problem solved! Have a happy stress free life!

If I was to ask an audience by a show of hands to designate what is currently causing stress in their lives the answers would come from both internal and external reasons. Both types of problems have a way of stealing your focus, energy and motivation. External reasons would be from the following areas.

- Relationships
- Work related
- Financial
- Health issues

External reasons come from every place imaginable. The kids won't stop screaming, your boss has been hounding you because you turned a report in late, and you owe the IRS thousands of dollars you don't have. The result is that you're seriously stressed out. Everyone has different stress triggers in their life. Out of all of these it seems that work stress tops the list, according to surveys. Forty percent of U.S. workers admit to experiencing office stress, and one-quarter say work is the biggest source of stress in their lives.

But sometimes the stress comes from inside, rather than outside. You can stress yourself out just by worrying about things. All of the following factors can lead to stress:

- Fear and uncertainty
- Attitudes and perceptions
- Unrealistic expectations
- Change in and around your life

Each, whether external or internal, can represent major obstacles that can stop you from having a happy outlook on life. Fifty percent of adults in our society have faced the agony of divorce. Then there is the devastation that comes from addictions. Bereavement from loss of a loved one as well as other types of losses take their toll, leaving emotional wreckage and scar tissue. Drive down any neighborhood street and I guarantee every home has faced major dilemmas and challenges. The fact is that no one is exempt.

The question is, what can we do about it and how can we turn these negatives into positives so we can get on with life?

This book was written to provide you with new perspectives and tools that you can put to work in your life. The action you take as a result of reading this book has a capacity to alter any human circumstance. The end result can be rewarding as you begin to once again see what is indeed possible for your life.

Chapter One

The Setting of the Sail

Author/Speaker Jim Rohn once used the analogy that the same wind blows upon each of us. The winds of difficulty as well as the winds of opportunity and breakthrough blow equally and in various ways. Take for instance, the story of a young couple who were excited about giving birth. This, their first pregnancy, had gone fairly well with no complications. When two ultrasounds were performed the doctors told the couple both times that everything was looking fine and that they were going to have a healthy baby boy.

The hospital room was bustling; the time for delivery had finally come. The final command to push came as the Father stood by reassuring his wife that she could do it and that they were almost there. With one final push the baby appeared. At first the mother could not see the baby. The first question she asked was, "Is the baby alright?" There was silence. As the seconds ticked by the mother sensed that something was wrong. Doctors crowded around and took the baby to the other side of the room for careful examination.

The dad, however, looked to see what was happening and noticed that their newborn baby boy had an arm missing. He suddenly had a rush of emotion flood over him as tears began to well up in his eyes. Feeling queasy and dizzy at the same time, he stumbled forward.

Perhaps, he thought to himself, I am mistaken, did I see what I think I saw? A nurse reached out to steady him and helped him out of the room.

The mother then knew there was something wrong. "What is it, what is wrong with my baby?" she demanded. The doctor hesitated at first but finally answered, "Phocamelia." A condition when a baby is born malformed or missing limbs.

Outside the door, the dad, with a look of concern, waited to hear the news as the pediatrician walked up to him. "Did I see what I thought I saw, my son has no arm?"

"Actually," the pediatrician said as carefully as he could, "your son has no arms and no legs."

I don't know about you, but that news had to be devastating. I am sure, a whole new set of questions came to the minds of these first time parents, "How are we to take care of this child?", "What possible good can ever come from this situation?" Have you ever felt like giving up - that somehow life's obstacles were just too much to handle - where you felt you were at the end of your rope?

Years later a young adolescent Nick Vujicic became despondent and depressed at his own plight. "How can anyone with no arms and no legs survive or have any value in this world?" he wondered. It was apparent that he would never have a girl friend to love him, a job, or later in years a wife. If he was to ever have a child, he would not be able to hold that child. He even thought that he wouldn't even be able to commit suicide if he wanted to. Who would pull the trigger?

The wind blows the same for all of us, as Jim Rohn put it. But in the case of the Vujicic family it was extra difficult and certainly could have had a more negative ending. We have seen marriages break apart over much less then what they had to endure. The Vujicic's attributed their success to a strong faith in God which gave them hope throughout the years ahead that somehow all things would work out for the good.

Whether they realized it or not, they also learned something else which Jim talks about in one of his speeches called *The Setting of The Sail*, which provides a very valuable lesson to us. Jim tells his audiences that all of us are in what is like a small sailboat and as everyone who sails knows, what determines the destination of the sailboat is not the blowing of the wind but the setting of the sail.

The wind shows up in all of our lives in various ways, the wind of disaster, the wind of opportunity and the wind of change. The wind when everything seems to be upside down, the wind when it is favorable as well as when it is unfavorable. The same wind blows on all of us, the economic wind, the social wind, even the political wind. Jim reinforces that the difference of arrival sites is not determined by the blowing of the wind, but by the setting of the sail.

What is the setting of the sail? Jim says that it is your philosophy in life that is the determining factor. In my own personal opinion I believe that part of that philosophy is the understanding that the wind is the same for each of us. Therefore, we cannot point to any one thing that is going on in our lives as the cause for where we happen to find ourselves in life. I realize that this concept or philosophy can be difficult to accept at first, it runs counter to how most people think about where their true problems and difficulties lie. Some may point to the storm winds of a bad financial news report as reason for failure, others may try to convince us that their reason for failure and struggle was past neglect or abuse.

Again, I am not here to trivialize any hardship or difficulty a person may be facing. But setting the sail means examining your philosophy in life. Your winning philosophy can mean your accepting personal responsibility and not falling into the quicksand of "the blame game." It can mean your attitude in life as well as your source of happiness.

This sounds easier said than done, doesn't it.

Nick Vujicic could have simply given into the winds of being born without limbs. Most people would not have blamed him one bit if he simply chose to accept his circumstances as the determining factor of his destination. He could have easily played the victim and become like the poor sailor who blames the wind for where he ends up.

Instead, Nick has gone on to become an international speaker, speaking to countless schools, churches, prisons, orphanages, hospitals, stadiums and in face-to-face encounters with individuals, telling them how very precious they are to God. He is a source of inspiration for thousands.

It is our greatest pleasure to assure people that God does have a plan for each and every life that is meaningful and purposeful! I am sure Nick would agree when I say the following. What people would count as a loss or as a mistake, God turns it for good and provides us with new perspective about what is possible for our lives. Set your sail with some of the basic truths in the following pages and you can change your destination.

ACTION STEPS:

Watch the following 8 minute video:
www.tinyurl.com/lifeafterlimbs

Based on the above video:

What were the two choices that Nick was presented with?

Where does healing and completeness take place?

"Obstacles are sometimes hard to overcome; they can cause people to quit trying, or they can cause people to develop more determination than ever!"

~ Jan Ross

Chapter Two

The Grand Design

Life can change in an instant. Sometimes it's the result of a chance encounter, or the reading of a letter discovered at the bottom of a jewelry box; sometimes it comes with the turning of a key, or even the purchase of a book. And sometimes it happens over office supplies.

Take for example, Sean Sessums, a young man in his twenties working for Staples office supply. It all started with a chance meeting with Brian Kramer, a customer who was shopping for supplies and who happened to be an attorney. Sean, hoping to help Brian find the right office equipment, asked what Brian did for a living. When he discovered that he was an attorney, Sean asked Brian for help with something his Mother had recently revealed to him.

You see, Sean's mother, Karen, at barely 18 and a teller at a Bank of America in Venice, California, had met Jack, a drummer who played gigs with local bands. The relationship did not last, but as a result, Sean was born. It wasn't until many years later that Karen revealed to her son Sean that he was a descendant of the Dukes — the legendary North Carolina clan that helped launch the American tobacco industry. At some point Karen learned that Jack received money from the large trust established for certain relatives of James B. Duke, Jack's great-great-great-uncle.

Brian Kramer agreed to help reunite Sean with his Father, which eventually took place. Chances are, Sean Sessums is now the wealthiest Staples clerk in America. All told, he says, he was granted a settlement from the Trust that should be worth several million dollars over the course of his life.

What young Sean found was not only reunification with his Father, he also discovered and eventually laid claim to an inheritance because of his heritage as a Duke. I am not certain to what degree this will affect the direction of Sean's life but if I know human nature, it would at least put a new swagger in your step. Hopefully the knowledge that you were born from noteworthy parents, grandparents or even great grandparents would give you a new appreciation about the choices and direction for your life.

We have all heard of the term, born for greatness. It is true, each of us have a world of possibility in front of us. Another thing that is similar is someone who was born from greatness. Being born from greatness suggests that a person comes from a linage with some type of meaning behind it. There could be a pedigree of royalty or some important accomplishment by a distant relative as in Sean's story.

Where you came from is an important consideration. For example, many people who are not able to conceive a child for one reason or another turn to a sperm bank where they can be inseminated. Careful selection of the father's background has become an important part of the process. Most scientists now recognize that intelligence is at least 50% determined by inheritance, and many would place that number closer to 70%. Such traits as musical ability, artistic talent, athletic aptitude, and many more talents are also partly genetic.

You Came From Greatness

Did you know that you are a carrier of greatness? When God created the earth, it contained the seeds that brought forth life. When He spoke and commanded the earth to bring forth plants, it did so because the seed was already there. When God created you, He placed seeds of greatness in you. Part of the reason that many of us don't realize that we carry seeds of greatness is because we've had so many negative things happen to us. God's plans and purposes (seeds of greatness) for our lives have become buried and or they are dormant, waiting for the right Words of Life to germinate them into action.

I believe that every human ever born came from that same greatness! The DNA of God's life force runs deep in you and if you allow the seeds of his goodness to grow in you, there is no way you will ever lose. God's intention for you can be seen in some of the first words in the Bible, "And God said, let them be fruitful and multiply". Being fruitful means to have increase, multiplication and growth. Mankind's ability to be resilient and fruitful against all odds is apparent throughout history.

I don't know what your concept of God may be, but I see Him as someone who deeply cares about each of us and has given us the ability to live a rich full life no matter the circumstances.

Isn't it interesting that we live in a world that in many ways does not amplify this? Millions of people today have no knowledge that they were born from greatness. Rather they are told that the human race came from a slithering amoeba crawling up out of the recesses of the sea. Could it be that we are afraid to embrace our linage because it calls us to a higher level?

There are three very important principles that will affect your mindset regarding your life.

1. What you think about God
2. What you think about yourself
3. What you think about your world

Although this is not a book on religion, it is important to note that our concept of God plays an important role in our personal lives. Dr. Timothy R. Jennings, M.D. states in his book *The God Shaped Brain*, that what you believe about God actually changes your brain.

Brain research in neuroscience has found that our thoughts and beliefs affect our physical, mental and spiritual health. Mind and body are interrelated, and we are designed for healthy relationships of love and trust. When we understand God as good and loving, we flourish. Unfortunately, many of us have distorted images of God and mostly think of him in fearful, punitive ways. This leads us into unhealthy patterns of self-defeating behaviors and toxic relationships.

Our belief about God naturally affects our view about ourselves. Am I loveable, am I validated and even more important does my significance come from God or will it come from the world around me. This leads us to the question, what do you believe is God's view and opinion of you?

What we think about our world can have great consequence on our lives. If my life is dependent on the dictates of the world around me then I am also a victim of that world. However, if I have the belief that I have been empowered to live a rich full purposeful life I will naturally receive the results. Unfortunately most people's personal identity and significance is dependent on a world that is constantly in flux. This opens us up to emotional sink holes and if we are not careful they can cause us to begin to find identity and significance in our misery and pain.

ACTION STEPS:

Imagine the end result of how you want your life to look.

Get it out of your head onto paper. Write it and mind map it out with pictures representing the desired end.

Create a book of desired outcomes for your life. "This is Me", This is who God created me to be.

Find others who are doing what it is you want to do and achieve.

"Pain is inevitable, suffering is not"

~Jim Richards

Chapter Three

The Power of Identity

Identity, purpose and design are some of the most important topics we can explore. When we are in harmony with our original design we soar, when we are out of harmony we struggle with life's challenges. It is commonly understood that identity is built on many things. Influences from our past experiences, our family, as well as peers help to form our identities. We look outside ourselves to establish and confirm our value. If those things outside of ourselves tell us that we are inept and powerless, then we become paralyzed where it concerns living a fulfilled life. However, if we find mirrored back to us that we have value and can contribute to our world out of that value, we then live a life of fulfillment and purpose. Living contributing out of our value rather than looking to our world for value is an important distinction.

One of the great lessons I learned years ago had to do with my intrinsic value being misplaced. This is where most people struggle. What is intrinsic value? It is the inherent value and worth of a thing. It is the value and worth that you have as God's creation. Its value and worth is not based on any outside influence whatsoever, it is not dependent upon view and opinion. My wife, new born infant and I had moved to Little Rock, Arkansas to attend a school whose emphasis was to send their graduates to other countries as missionaries. After graduating we were excited about the next step in our journey. We had decided that the Philippines were the place we were to go. We raised monthly support from friends and family and were sent out to work with the only Philippine contact the school had. After arriving and spending a month or two getting use to the new culture, we sat down with Tom, the church contact we had been sent to work with. He told us that we were to take over a church in the Mindanao area. We were assured that the person who we were to replace was moving to another location and would not be returning, so we would be free to do whatever we saw necessary.

A few months later, after arriving at the church and working closely with the nationals, the church body began to experience growth. We all celebrated the progress that was being made. Unfortunately, jealousy from the person whose position we had replaced became a problem. The woman was over five hundred miles away, but false stories were circulated about our progress, and complaints were made to the home office. Eventually we were confronted by the home office and threatened that our support was going to be discontinued. We were not asked about our side of the story and were not allowed to refute it whatsoever.

This was devastating to me personally. We thought we had found our life's work and were excited about our future. We felt rejected and abandoned by the very people with whom we had spent a year in training. I felt that not only they had deserted us, but worse yet,

God had failed us. We did not have enough funds for the three of us to return to the United States so I sent Debra home ahead with our one year old son. It wasn't until a month later that I was able to raise the additional funds to get myself back to the United States and join my family.

Why do I share this story with you? Because of the effects this experience had on me over the next five years. I was emotionally devastated. I was angry, depressed and became self-destructive. As for Debra, she was disappointed, but not to the degree that I was. I often wondered later why that was, which eventually led me to the following conclusion.

Unknowingly, I had built my identity upon the shifting sands of man's opinion. Those who had sent us were to be esteemed, but were never meant to be my source. I did not understand that the opinions of others and obstacles in life did not define me, my intrinsic value defined me.

Build your life upon the opinion of others and the level of your feeling of success and your identity and you will be certain to eventually fall into despair. People find their identities in many things, such as their relationships with others, a spouse, or even a child. Others find their personal worth and value in the house they live in, the car, the plaque on the wall, or their job.

I'm not saying it is wrong to have feelings of pride about your accomplishments or to feel good about the relationships in your life. What I am saying is that if you go into a relationship looking to that person to make you feel worth and value, you will soon destroy that relationship because you sucked all the life out of the other person by expecting them to meet a need that no human can meet.

A successful marriage is not when two people come together, each representing 50% of the value to add to the other in order to make each other feel complete. I promise that a marriage built on this idea will never work. Why? The reason it won't work is because neither person will ever measure up to the expectations of the other.

However, if you come into a relationship realizing that you have incredible intrinsic value and worth, you soon realize that you are already 100% whole. The end result is powerful and freeing! I am not talking about having an egotistical attitude that is demanding. This type of person is only acting out of their own lack of value and personal worth. A person who actually realizes his or her own intrinsic value can see the value of others and share intimately without demanding or offering more than they should.

Why do we forget about our intrinsic value? Our experiences speak so loudly to us through our five senses that we begin to define ourselves by them. There are two great lies that try to define who we are. The voice of our past experiences tries to define our value and as a result we succumb to the lie that tells us that we no longer have any choices because we are the end result of our past negative experiences.

The second lie concerns what we are experiencing in the present. We look for validation from the externals of our world. We use the relationships, positions, possessions in our lives to prove to ourselves and others that we have value and worth. Because our life is built on what we are experiencing when things go wrong, we think that we are wrong. We believe that we no longer have any other choice than to be miserable and stuck because we believe that the negatives surrounding our lives are somehow controlling us.

In some instances, if we are not careful we can fall into the trap of feeling validated by our pain. In psychology this is called secondary gain. Secondary gain keeps us stuck because we are using our pain to meet our needs for value and worth. "If I lay here long enough in my misery, somebody will come by and feel sorry for me." Nick Vujicic discovered a worth that came from a loving God. He didn't quite know why his handicap happened to him and could have blamed God himself as a reason not to get on with living life. Instead, he found value, love and worth, which turned into purpose and passion that is touching the world. He saw that he had value beyond his having no arms and no legs. It was a value that could never be exhausted in its service to mankind.

ACTION STEPS:

Write a paragraph, or two, that answers the following questions:

- Why must you achieve your ultimate vision?
- What is your ultimate purpose for your life? What will it give you to achieve this vision in your life? How will that make you feel?
- Ultimately, why do you want to achieve your vision?
- Whose lives will you touch in the process?
- What is the purpose that would drive you to push through anything that might try to hold you back?
- How would it feel to achieve the ultimate vision for your life?
- What emotions do you want to experience as a result?

_____

*"Inside of every person there is greatness;
there is a winner just trying to get out"*

_____

Chapter Four

How To Respond To Difficulty

The obituary read; Died of natural causes. My immediate question was, at age 53 how can anything be called natural? My wife Debra and I hadn't heard from Marilyn or her son Brandon for over 10 years. The news of her passing was a complete shock to the both of us! We knew Marilyn those many years ago as a person who was a bright and optimistic person who always looked forward to the future with hope. Her trust in God was always apparent even in times of difficulty. Now, Marilyn was gone, poof, vanished. What could have happened to cause such a young life to be taken from us?

Brandon, her son explained to me that there was a lot of stress that was taking place in her life in the last few years and as a result started drinking. She had recognized that she had a problem and submitted herself to AA about 5 years ago. She had just finished a sixty day sober living home program and was doing well. In fact, she was planning on becoming an AA counselor herself. She had a passion for helping people handle their own demons. But at age 53 something tragic happened that changed everything.

After 30 years working as a dietary supervisor she lost her job and benefits unfairly. For the next six months Marilyn fought to get her job back but eventually the stress killed her. Marilyn's story although tragic is not exclusive to her. We live in a world where not everything goes the way we plan. If we were honest with ourselves I think you would agree that rarely things go the way we want them to go.

If you are a parent, children make choices that are beyond your control. If you're an employee there is the possibility of becoming unemployed. A couple starts out in life falling in love with each other and in the end go through a devastating divorce.

The question of emotional stability comes into play at every turn in life. Have you seen the television commercial where the senior citizen cry's out, "Help I've fallen and I can't get up?" The mantra of our day seems to be, "Help I'm emotionally stressed out and I'm not going to survive." Truth be told, No one and I mean no one, gets a free "get out of jail" card where it concerns difficulties and challenges in life.

Our parents and grandparents knew stress. They grew up in cold water hovels with an outhouse during the depression. They collected coal from the train tracks to keep warm. They then went to a war that ate up their generation. They came home and learned about bomb shelters, and then went to war again.

Life living and making a living is about the choices we are making regarding how we see ourselves; it is about our focus and belief that all things are possible no matter the obstacle, difficulty or challenge. Realize that ultimately it is you who must set the sail of your boat in regard to your destination.

Someone once wrote: Those whose names are worth remembering never lived a life of ease. It is true! Every great story of accomplishment that we read or hear about came out of places of difficulty, tragedy and apparent defeat.

Just take a look at a few I've listed here.

Nelson Mandela (1918 - 2013) worked very hard to train as a lawyer, despite the South African apartheid system making this very difficult for a black man.

Against the odds Nelson Mandela was able to practice law, helping many black South Africans to survive in the apartheid system. When Nelson Mandela was sent to jail for his opposition to apartheid in the 1960s, there seemed no end in sight to the all-powerful apartheid system of South Africa. But, against the odds, Mandela played a critical role in bringing about the end of apartheid and the first truly democratic elections.

Helen Keller (1880-1968) became deaf & blind before her second birthday. Despite this debilitating disability, she learned to read and write, and became the first deaf blind person to gain a bachelor degree. She campaigned on issues of social welfare, women's suffrage, disability rights and impressed many with her force of personality.

J.K.Rowling became the world's bestselling children's author, despite managing on benefits from the government as a single mother. Initially, her manuscript for Harry Potter was rejected by several publishers.

Rosa Parks could have easily been just another statistic in the American system of racial segregation.

Thomas Edison was fired from his job, when a chemical experiment, leaked acid on to his boss's desk. However, despite being almost penniless, Edison rose to be the most prolific inventor of his generation.

Nick Vujicic is an amazing story about a baby boy born without limbs. He has gone on to achieve many things that would seem impossible. He has a loving wife, a child an international speaking business and ministry that is touching thousands of lives around the world.

Your story isn't any different!

The obstacles you face, the frustrations and fears that crowd your mind are no different from those faced by millions of others around you The winds of life's difficulties are no different for any of us yet one lands successfully at their destination while the other becomes shipwrecked. What guides us to different destinations in life is determined by the setting of the sail. The way that each of us thinks makes the major difference in where each of us arrives.

These amazing stories tell each of us that we are capable of much more than we believe we are capable of achieving.

Miracles Still Happen

Looking back over our lives, I realize that many miracles have taken place. Most were the result of taking action in the midst of impossible situations. For instance, three years ago we decided to accept an invitation to travel to Uganda, Africa where we were to speak at a minister's conference. Because we were going to a developing country we knew that they really didn't have the money to pay for our trip, we would have to raise the money ourselves.

We carefully checked airline prices which included traveling to Heathrow Airport in London to Kenya, Africa and finally to Entebbe, Uganda. Our estimation for the total trip meant we would have to raise $5,000. We immediately went to work, I put a Facebook page up about our goal, and we talked to people and shared our vision for going.

As we approached the date of our time to leave we found that we had a dilemma. We were just seven days away from leaving and we had only raised $1,000. We hadn't been able to pay for our tickets yet and quite frankly we were at the end of our rope. We were embarrassed to go back to those who had helped us thus far and tell them that we had failed. We were also concerned about the host pastor who had put his own time, money and effort into preparation for us to come.

We shared our problem with someone we knew from our church. She was from Kenya and thought she could shed some light on whether she thought our host's would be disappointed and would be able to cancel without creating too many problems or issues.

Helen, our Kenyan friend did not hesitate one moment in her answer to us. She emphatically said, "Do not give up! You are going; you watch, the money will come!" On our way home that night we talked and decided that somehow, no matter what, we were going. Although it looked quite impossible we chose to believe that God would make a way.

We got out of bed that next morning and something extraordinary happened. The phone began to ring, "Hello Scott? Yes, my wife and I want to help you get to Uganda, we want to send you $100." It wasn't just one call, it was many who called us out of nowhere wanting to help us. Suddenly sales for my online business took a spike. Complete strangers from different parts of the world came to the website that I had set up to receive donations and began to give. Places like Europe, New Zealand, as well as the Caribbean. Within twenty four hours we went online and purchased our tickets and just six days later we found ourselves standing in the Denver International Airport with our bags ready to board for the trip of a life time.

What did we learn from this experience? Choosing to make changes in our life is not always easy. We wanted to make a difference in those we were going to touch in Uganda and it took courage for us to step out and go for our dream. We also discovered the power of what can take place when you sell out to a direction and dream for your life.

The easiest time to quit is when things look hopeless, but truth be told, it is your greatest opportunity to press through. I never want to trivialize the difficulties anyone may be facing. These are real issues that can become stumbling blocks that keep us from living a full productive life. At the same time, the above stories prove that there is a world of possibility hiding in your own personal story.

It is my desire to encourage, assist and coach you toward seeing a world of possibility in the midst of life's challenges. Will it be easy? Let's just say that it will be easier, once you become intentional about your life and the direction you want to go. Over time you will establish new patterns that will support you in living a more resilient, purposeful life.

One of the primary motivations for writing this book is to assist readers in their efforts to recapture and develop their authority, esteem and initiative in life. As a result they can experience more happiness, peace of mind and prosperity.

ACTION STEPS:

We are each motivated by pleasure and move away from what is considered painful. Avoiding the pain in our lives stops us from taking action and making choices we need to make.

You can change the dynamics of this in a powerful way by taking a piece of paper and drawing a line down the middle. On the top write in a sentence the obstacle and decision you are struggling with. On the left side of the vertical line write the word, PLEASURE and on the top right side, write the word PAIN.

Under the word pleasure, make a list of all the positive results that will take place if you indeed make the choice to move forward in your life regarding this issue.

Go to the right side and under the word pain and write down a list of things that will result if you don't make the necessary choices to move forward in your life regarding this issue.

Taking the above action step is a powerful way to change the dynamics of how to motivate you to take action. It uses basic physiological principles that are continually at work in our lives.

"You are not here merely to make a living. You are here to enable the world to live more amply, with greater vision, and with a finer spirit of hope and achievement. You are here to enrich the world. You impoverish yourself if you forget this errand."

~ Woodrow Wilson

Chapter Five

Feelings and Emotions

Imagine yourself entering a room where perhaps forty or so other people are waiting. As you enter to find an open seat, you look around and notice that most of the others are about the same age as you. Most of the people in the room seem pretty average and moderately dressed. As you are sitting down someone hands you two sheets of paper with bold words across the top that say "A List of Feelings".

As you study the sheets there are a long list of words divided into columns. A quick math count down one column times how many columns there are, tells you that there are approximately 198 words listed. The list comprises many feelings using descriptive words of all kinds. You see the words "annoyed" and with a deep sigh you think to yourself, yeah I guess I'm a little annoyed right now because I want this seminar to get started and then you chuckle at yourself.

Here is a small sampling of what you see:

Grateful	Stimulated	Durable
Anxious	Focused	Relieved
Defiant	Frustrated	Elated
Evasive	Detached	Secure
Cautious	Numb	Confident
Useful	Committed	Numb
Jealous	Accepted	Effective
Impatient	Bright	Depressed
Denied	Confused	Neglected
Eager	Inadequate	Delighted
Enriched	Aggressive	Blessed
Ignorant	Annoyed	Alone

A gentleman enters the front of the room and after welcoming everyone, he instructs everybody to go through the list of words and circle the feelings they are experiencing at the moment.

You look at the two sheets and let out a quiet sigh of agony, but decide to do what he says because after all you paid for this class. Let's see, how about the word annoyed for starters and you circle the word. Chuckling to yourself, you then circle the word amused! In about five minutes you finish the list and look around the room to see if anyone else was done.

If you attended one of our workshop seminars, this is part of what you would experience. What is interesting is that although each person in the same room is experiencing and participating in the same event, each sheet in the room would be completely different. At some level one would think that this would be irrational. Same stimulus, same experience should mean same feelings, but that is not true. One person may be excited to be in the room while the person sitting next to them is unsettled or anxious.

Everyone there was having the same experience, at the same time, with the same speaker up front, everything is essentially the same. The question is, then, why would there be such a wide variety of feelings between attendees? The evidence here shows us that we are carrying the past and the future around with us. It is that influence that is creating how we feel at any given moment.

This is why at times we feel completely out of command of our feelings and emotions. We allow how we are feeling at the time to dominate our posture to the rest of the world. This is true in our place of work with co-workers or even with other family members living in the same home. We are each experiencing the same things at the same time but are having a different outcome where it concerns our feelings.

Take the story of Judy and Bob for example. Judy, now married with two children, was raised as a foster child. She has dealt with vast emotional swings that seem to come out of a deep sense of insecurity. Her husband is at a total loss of knowing how to make her happy.

For example, Valentine's Day comes and he is up early to take care of the children so Judy can enjoy the morning sleeping in. He goes to the store and comes back with flowers, candy, and carrot cake, which is her favorite. With anticipation he cooks a beautiful breakfast and brings it all to the bedroom to surprise her.

Judy immediately rejects the gifts he brings to her because it makes her feel inadequate. Instead of saying thank you, she complains that she is on a diet and she won't eat. He feels like she is rejecting him and takes everything back out of the room.

She knows that she can't reciprocate and somehow feels powerless. She now feels angry because he simply walked away, telling him "At least you could have left the flowers and candy." She feels like she is the victim and as a result acts out by pushing back and blaming Bob for making her feel bad.

Most people don't realize that they have choices where it concerns their feelings. This is because they have abdicated this part of their lives to the sub-conscious mind. The sub-conscious is that part of the brain that handles all the things the conscience brain doesn't want to do, like breathing and keeping our heart beating. Have you ever driven somewhere and you don't remember how you got there or had routines that you go through without any conscious thought?

One of the primary functions of the sub-conscious mind is to keep us safe. This means it will resist things it interprets as out of the ordinary. Think of it like a fence around your house, a boundary line of sorts.

If the boundary line is crossed where it concerns new choices and directions in your life your sub-conscious will create resistance. Resistance can come in many forms. For instance, your physiology changes where you feel sick or have sweaty palms when asked to speak in front of a crowd, or perhaps you are losing weight with a diet plan or an exercise regimen and then for some reason or other you suddenly give up because of some excuse that crept up in your mind.

Anything that is outside of what the sub-conscious deems as normal can create resistance. This includes the level of chaos you allow or disallow in your life or even the standard of living you seem to be stuck at. The bottom line is that if you are not making conscious choices about your life and feelings, your sub-conscious will assume that what you are experiencing is normal and will automatically run your life and feelings for you on auto pilot. In the end this creates the illusion that you don't have control or choices over specific areas of your life.

The Power of a Feelings List

If you are in the habit of reaching for negative feelings, you will tend to blame outside influences as the reason, like Judy who blames her husband for the way she feels.

Using a feelings list to help her identify how she feels once or twice a day would help her consciously think about and identify feelings more clearly. This simple act would bring a new awareness to her and better choices could be established over time.

Let me help you narrow down your feelings list. I propose that while there are thousands of feelings from moment to moment, there are only two basic emotions, love and fear. By understanding the emotion that is more in alignment with the feeling you are experiencing, you can better understand the feeling and take appropriate measures. The question then become one of two choices. Am responding and acting out of love or am I responding and acting out of fear?

It simply makes it that much more apparent and helps us to be more conscious that we can make better choices in our lives.

Here is an example from our above list of feelings that shows how they can be categorized:

LOVE	FEAR
Grateful	Anxious
Useful	Defiant
Eager	Evasive
Enriched	Cautious
Stimulated	Ignorant
Focused	Frustrated
Accepted	Confused

Emotions are a mental or psychological state while feelings tend to describe a physical manifestation of emotions.

At any given moment throughout the day each of us are experiencing hundreds of different feelings. Let's take a closer look at these feelings by examining the feelings on the below graph. Each peak and valley represents a moment by moment experience.

A typical moment can be represented as simply a second or two before moving into the next moment.

Perhaps your first peak of the day is the sound of laughter of a child outside your window, and your glance out the window to get a better view results in a smile. The first valley or negative feeling is when you do glance out the window you also wonder if those clouds are going to bring a storm in. The second peak is the smell of a fresh brewed pot of coffee you had earlier started. The next valley could have been the disruption of the phone ringing. You then feel excited because the call is from a friend and you want to share an exciting idea. Your feelings of excitement become the third peak but then because your friend suddenly has to hang up, and you feel slighted and put-off.

Have you ever met anyone that represented the below feelings graph? This is someone who constantly reaches for fear based feelings.

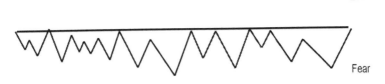

The above graph reminds me of someone we use to know. Every time we would meet it was completely miserable. She would tell us about all her woes and how life was badly treating her. She would complain about having to take care of her aging Father who was living with her. At different times she would even express to us how she wished her Father would die.

What she was experiencing was real to her, and no doubt was difficult. Her life hadn't been easy and she was in a bad situation having to take care of her ailing Father. What she didn't understand was that she did have choices. Her Father was not the issue even though she believed him to be. Then our circumstances changed and we didn't see her for some time. A year later we saw her at the store. After greeting her we asked, "How is your Father doing?" She told us that he had passed on a few months back. She went on to tell us how difficult her life since his death had been and that she just didn't know what she was going to do. Obviously her sub-conscious mind accepted this as her normal and as a result she truly believed that she had no other choice but to be miserable.

The following feelings graph is the most optimal way to live but not very probable for a lot of people. Experiencing love on continual bases takes practice.

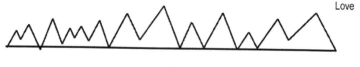

Love

Fear

Love is the opposite of fear. Love is focused on making a difference in the world outside of me. I am caring and in a state of contribution to those around me. Fear is always self-focused. When I am in fear I am most likely in a survival mode, which means I am constantly in fight, flight or freeze responses physically and emotionally.

When I am in a flight survival mode, I tend to withdraw from the world. When I am in a fight mode, I am angry and ready to strike out at those around me. Getting outside of yourself is one of the fastest ways of getting out of a survival mode. Taking action means changing your focus from a "poor me" complex and finding a place where you can make a contribution. For instance, writing this book is an act of love, I am actually sitting here thinking of you and how I can communicate to you in such a way that I can make a difference in your life.

There are many ways you can do this, simply by changing your perceptions about how you are serving others at your place of work. You might volunteer at your church, synagogue or at a public-service organization.

Recently I read the story Richard Paul Evans shared in his book *The Four Doors*. The event took place when his children were young. His seven year old daughter Abigail had just learned how to swim but was still fearful of the deep water. Abigail decided to play it safe and chose to stay in the shallow end of the pool. At the same time, her three year old brother Michael, who couldn't swim, was wearing arm floaters and was able to swim in the deep end.

Richard was sitting on a lounge chair at the side of the pool when Abi began to shout. He looked over and saw her in the deep end of the pool holding onto Michael's arm, struggling to keep her head above water.

"Abi!" he shouted. "Let go of him!" The two continued to struggle. Again shouting, "Abi!" "You're going to drown both of you! Let go of him right now!" At that moment the lifeguard jumped into the pool and pulled the two children out of the water. It was only then that Richard learned what had actually happened.

Michael had jumped into the pool with his arms extended above his head. One of his floaters had slipped completely off while the other one had slid up to his elbow. As a result Michael became partially submerged under the water. Abigail had jumped in to save her brother. Her selfless love was stronger than her fear.

Never underestimate the power of selfless love in its ability to extinguish fear.

Overcoming Emotional Barriers

Overcoming emotional barriers in your life is perhaps the most difficult step you will take in your life. I know how difficult it can be to get past anger, guilt, anxiety and loss of esteem. Here some helpful steps you can apply right now.

Create a new Habit of letting go when you find your mind dwelling and meditating on the problem – This means, stop clinging to regrets and playing old tapes in your head. This could concern a divorce, loss of a job, or loss of a loved one. Whatever it is, let it go! It will help to physically "let go" or to "send it away" or even dig a hole and bury it if need be. I know of one woman who was going through a divorce and she literally dug a hole and buried her wedding dress.

Focus on your strengths. Begin to focus on what you do have, not on what you don't have. Create a list of strengths that will create evidence to support where you want to go. Practice counting your blessings continually.

Practice Meditation. You are either meditating on the good or you are meditating on the bad. Finding a place of solitude and peace is a powerful place to live. Take time each night or as soon as you wake to contemplate "I am" statements about how you see yourself. See yourself experiencing the life you want in the present tense.

ACTION STEPS:

Go to the following web link and listen to the 6 minute audio.
www.52lifelessons.com/life21.php

This audio introduces the concept of imprinting and how it can affect us.

---

*"What you are is God's gift to you, what you
become is your gift to God & the world."*

~ Hans Urs von Balthasar

Chapter Six

How Fear Stopped Me

Fear stopped me for years; I was paralyzed and frustrated, even depressed at times. I felt stifled in many areas of my life. I found it difficult to make phone calls, talk to people or make simple steps in life that would have opened doors of opportunity for me. The end result was that I hid from the world and life around me.

What are your biggest fears?

Your emotions are birthed from your thoughts, what you concentrate on. Take for example when you are watching a horror movie. As you watch, your emotions react as if you are really experiencing what you are watching. Your heart will race, your hands will sweat, and your whole body will tremble and feel the fear.

This is because your emotions cannot judge truth or reality, they only manifest your thoughts. We know that if this is happening when watching a movie on a screen then it must be true if you think and meditate on things that are pleasant. The end result will be that you will begin to experience and manifest pleasant emotions.

There is a force that stands between you and your destiny. It is an adversary so strong that it is capable of causing reason and wisdom to flee as it drives us to the brink of unbelief.

Our deadly opponent is FEAR, which is also an acronym for False Evidence Appearing Real. Fear is disempowering to the degree that you yield to its deception. Imaginary fears can become so real to you that if you believe in them they manifest. Even the most unfounded ones can alter the course of our lives and in time change our destiny.

Stress tends to visit us when we are tired, sick, driving through a crowded metropolis, when we are late to a meeting, have taken on too many responsibilities. When circumstances are out of our control our basic needs are not being met and our safety is threatened.

Fear and Stress is the number one cause of disease, heart attacks, strokes, cancer, irritable bowel syndrome, mental break downs, and the list goes on. Our muscles tighten and do not allow the blood to flow through smoothly.

We cannot stop the fear and stress from coming, it happens every day through the TV shows and movies and news anchors who want us to know all the dangers of life. Our friends and family can also bring fear and stress to us. Other stressors may be things like driving in traffic, circumstantial changes, a doctor visit with negative news, raising a family and teenagers, as well as many other things.

As a wife and mom, I have faced many fearful situations, including the concern for a child's wellbeing after a fall and the stress of making ends meet at the end of the month.

One personal story took place when we lived in Sacramento, California back in 1980. Scott and I worked at a Bobby McGee's restaurant as janitors part time while we went to college.

Each morning we would arrive early, at 6 am, and open up the back door by the kitchen. One day, as we went to open the door as usual, a man suddenly appeared from behind a trash can. He had a woman's stocking pulled over his head and was holding a knife.

Our first reaction was to laugh at this silly looking guy with the stocking over his head. We laughed and laughed until a second guy came out from behind the same coke machine with a gun. That was when fear took over and I began to scream uncontrollably.

They must have thought I was totally crazy, laughing and then screaming. The paper boy who was in the area that morning delivering papers couldn't help but hear all the emotion I was displaying that early morning. As a result he called 911. Scott took control of the whole situation and pointed at me and told me to shut up, for fear that they might react and stab or shoot me. He then told these two thugs to put away their weapons and I would settle down. Little did we know that those two had recently been released from Folsom prison and were on parole.

Scott knew me well. Everyone acts differently when under stress and fear. I believe that under those circumstance whatever is in your heart will come out. I must have had both joy and fear because I laughed and screamed.

Demanding that we let them into the restaurant, they asked to be let into the room where the previous night's receipts were kept. We told them that we did not have keys and that the person who did would not be in until later that morning. That morning, stupid took over logic and reason for these two, because they decided to wait. They tied us up and placed us in the bathroom as they walked around the restaurant waiting for the bookkeeper to arrive so that they could force her to open up the safe. As we waited, we could hear them walking around and talking, at one point their gun must have gone off by accident because we heard a shot.

At the time we didn't know that the paperboy had heard my screams and the police had come and surrounded the restaurant outside (Thank you, paper boy, for being our hero). Once the thugs had noticed the police they got scared and wanted to run, but they needed us and our car for a getaway.

They didn't realize that our little green Pinto had mechanical issues. The starter had recently gone out and we were in the process of getting it fixed. Until that time we were getting by with what we had. We had been push-starting the car to get it started. I would help push from behind the car and Scott would push from the driver's side. Once the car got started rolling he would jump in and put it in gear.

When Scott told them about our car they said, "What? Now what are we going to do?" Scott, the counselor, explained to them that they hadn't up to that point done anything too bad, their only crime was breaking and entering. Scott continued to tell them that he would hide their weapons in the laundry basket so that the charges would be less. They actually believed everything and went along with everything that Scott had said.

Knowing and believing who you are gives you a strength and peace in all situations good and bad. They were probably more afraid then we were. We knew God was there with us and knew that everything would work out for the good. Looking back, I realized that if I focused on the situation I was overcome by fear but when I began to pray and turn my thoughts toward God and remind myself that He was with us, fear would lose its grip on me.

The robbers sent Scott out with a white napkin to surrender to the police for them, but the police didn't know that Scott was the hostage so they treated him like one of the robbers. They had him on the ground surrounding him with guns, as the police and swat team closed in to handcuff their suspect. As he laid on the ground with all the guns pointed at him he realized I was alone in the restaurant with both robbers. He thought to himself, what did I just do? She should have come out first and I should have stayed.

There I was, left with these two guys - who knew what could happen? Amazingly, the robbers began to apologize to me, giving me gum and realizing that this was a robbery gone wrong. They hid their weapons as Scott had suggested and one by one surrendered to the police.

I looked around at the mess in the restaurant waiting for me to clean it up. Instead of going outside I went back to work, picked up the vacuum and started cleaning. The police, wondering what had happened, took out their bullhorns and called for me to come out, but I couldn't hear them. I was busy, working away, happy that I was okay and everything turned out fine. Finally I turned and there were two policemen asking if I was okay and if I would come outside with them.

Later, we had to go to court as witnesses in the robbery. Their lawyer asked Scott while on the stand, "My client told me that you were not afraid and were calm during the occurrence." The attorney felt that by mentioning this he could sway the court that this was not as serious of a crime as it had really been. They had witnessed a peace, and yes, laughter in a situation that normally would have been cause for panic.

This story tells you that YES you can have and experience joy and Peace even in a fearful and stressful situation. Stuff happens every day, but when you have built a foundation of thoughts in your life that are pure lovely and of good report you will have an inner peace and joy that will show up on the outside. Your emotions will manifest what you are thinking on the inside.

ACTION STEPS:

Write down what you are afraid of and then on the next
Line next to it write down the opposite of your fear.

Example:

My Fear:

I have a fear of the phone
because I believe that I will
get yelled at and rejected by
the person on the other end.

I have a fear of spiders
because they might jump on
me.

I Choose To See:

I see people excited to talk to
me on the phone; they are
my friends and want what I
have to give or share with
them.

Spiders are more afraid of
me. They won't attack me,
they run from me because I
am bigger than they are.

"There are many things in life that will catch your eye, but only a few will catch your heart...pursue those."

~ Michael Nolan

Chapter Seven

Debra's Three Keys to Living a Joy-Filled Life

I have three tips that are guaranteed to work, and if you put these into practice every day in your life, you will not only see a change in your wellbeing and health but you will affect others around you as well.

1st Key - What Do You See?

"The Key to Success is to focus our conscious mind on things we desire, not things we fear." *Brian Tracy*

I asked my husband for the ten-thousandth time to make a phone call for me. You see, I was afraid of the phone! I would stumble and hesitate whenever I talked to someone on the phone and I just hated being in this position. I knew Scott wanted me to become more assertive, so he started saying no. "No, I will not make calls for you, you must do it yourself," he would say.

Wow! Now what was I going to do? Have you ever been afraid to make phone calls even to your own mother? That was me.

WHAT I SAW:

When I picked up the phone to talk, I would see angry, mad people on the other end of the phone. I didn't understand it at the time, but my mom had set up a pattern of fear in my life as I grew up. She always yelled at me when I bothered or called her. So I was afraid that if I made a phone call I would disturb someone or wake them up or make them angry.

So I had Scott make phone calls for me. I would think to myself that if he talks first then when he passed the phone to me I could be sure they would be in a good mood. Talk about someone who had irrational thinking!

This fear of the phone put me in a box. I was alone and full of fear. FUDs (fear, uncertainty and doubts) stopped me dead in my tracks. I would sit around and think that somehow if I wait for courage and confidence to come knocking on my door things would change. They didn't, instead, the more I thought about it, the more fear I had. I had built scary monsters in my head that were stopping me from growing.

SOMEONE COULD SEE ME

Ten years ago I accepted a job where I was forced to face my fears. One of my primary duties was to make phone calls. Joe Sabah, my employer and friend, saw something that I was not capable of seeing. He saw potential in me and helped me to see through a different set of eyes. Joe helped me by explaining to me and convincing me that the people on the other end of the phone line were not angry, they were my friends.

By simply changing my point of view about how people felt about me, I chose to see that people wanted to talk to in fact looked forward to my receiving my call. He taught me to turn my fear into action and see how the person at the other end of the phone was my friend.

He showed me how he saw me as a confident, bright woman full of joy and passion. Joe had me recognize that whenever I started a sentence with the words like "I can't...., I have to.... It's impossible to...." - that was a limiting belief .

Fear of failure, feelings of rejection, ridicule, the unknown, or mediocrity had kept me from pursuing activities or goals that might otherwise bring me success or joy. He gave me new glasses to wear. I eventually learned to love the phone and made 1000 phone calls for Joe's business every six months. I was making new friends every day I picked up that phone.

NOW I CAN SEE

I now have joy and have broken out of the box of fear over my life. I can communicate to the world in a way I never thought possible and as a result opportunities are now endless. The phone is no longer an obstacle or in my way, it is a door to opening up a new world in front of me.

ACTION STEP

Write down what you see

Write down what you want to see

_____

Have you had something stopping you from achieving your potential and destiny?

What do you see? What are you thinking about, will it be of fear or joy? Think about it for just a moment and you will probably come up with a common list of the "usual suspects" such as lack of education, lack of financial resources, lack of support, unexpected personal obstacles.

Fear of failure, rejection, ridicule, the unknown or mediocrity keeps us from pursuing activities or goals that might otherwise bring us success or joy. There is a scripture in the Bible that I had always referred to as a reminder to me.

Philippians 4:8 …"Finally, brethren, whatsoever
Things are true,
Things are honest,
Things are just,
Things are pure,
Things are lovely,
Things are of good report
If there be any virtue, and if there be any praise,

THINK ON THESE THINGS

Choose to Live overwhelmed by God's opinion of you which is Love. Ponder that which is of excellent virtue study stories that celebrate life. Refuse to dwell on or meditate on those things that are contrary to the positive.

2nd Key – Be Happy

Laughter is a powerful antidote to stress, pain and conflict. Nothing works faster or more dependably to bring your mind and body back into balance than a good laugh.

Humor lightens your burdens, inspires hope, connects you to others and keeps you grounded, focused and alert. Proverbs 15:15 says, "He who is of a merry heart has a continual feast." And also, "Proverbs 17:22, "A cheerful heart is good medicine" Experiencing a life of continual celebration is dependent on what is in the heart. The quality of our life, the thing that makes life abundant, this very "secret key," is in the joy of the heart.

There are benefits to you from laughter:

- It reduces stress,
- Lowers blood pressure
- Elevates mood
- Boosts the immune system
- Improves brain functioning
- Protects the heart

- Connects you to others
- Fosters instant realization
- Makes you feel good.

Humor enhances our ability to connect with others. When I laugh, I am replacing distressing, negative emotions with pleasurable feelings. When we experience humor we talk more, make more eye contact and touch others in positive ways. It is contagious.

When we laugh, our body relaxes and endorphins (natural painkillers) are released into the blood stream. Laughter Therapy was introduced by a Dr. Lee Berk of Loma University, who did a research study in 1970. He did an experiment on ten healthy people. Five test subjects watched a comedy show and five sat in a room doing nothing. He took blood samples of all ten afterwards and found cortisol (the hormone that our body releases when under stress) was stronger in the five who had done nothing than the five that sat through the comedy show.

Berk's research has also shown that the level of natural killer cells (a type of immune cell that attacks virus and tumor cells) is increased through laughter. These same cells are suppressed if the body suffers consistent long-term stress.

Our muscles relax when feeling of elation and joy is expressed. Our muscles tighten when feelings of fear and stress are expressed. 20 seconds of laughter is as good for the lungs as three minutes spent on a rowing machine

Benefits to Taking Your Daily Dose of Laughter

- Strengthen your immune system
- Boost your energy
- Diminish pain
- Protect you from the damaging effects of stress
- Best of all this priceless medicine is fun, free, and easy

The sound of roaring laughter is far more contagious than any cough, sniffle, or sneeze. When share it binds people together and increases happiness and intimacy. Laughter also triggers healthy physical changes in the body.

Create Opportunities to Laugh

Watch a funny movie or TV show
Go to a comedy club
Read the funny pages
Seek out funny people
Share a good joke or a funny story
Host game night with friends
Play with a pet
Go to a "Laughter yoga" class
Goof around with children
Be silly
Make time for fun activities (bowling, miniature golf, hiking, etc.)

When you incorporate more humor and play into your daily interactions it can improve the quality of your love relationships as well as your connections with co-workers, family members, and friends.

If you can learn to laugh in spite of the circumstances that surround you, you will enrich others, enrich yourself and more than that you will live long.

ACTION STEP

What do you do that creates Laughter for you?

_____

_____

"Celebrate God all day, every day. I mean, revel in him! Make it as clear as you can to all you meet that you're on their side, working with them and not against them. Help them see that the Master is about to arrive. He could show up any minute!" Philippians 4:4 (Message)

"A happy heart is good medicine and a cheerful mind works healing, but a broken spirit dries up the bones." Proverbs 17:22 (Amplified)

Consider it wholly joyful, my brethren, whenever you are enveloped in or encounter trials of any sort or fall into various temptations. James 1:2 (Amplified)

3rd Key – Gratitude

Numerous studies suggest that grateful people are more likely to have higher levels of happiness and lower levels of stress and depression

At times our own light goes out and is rekindled by a spark from another person. Each of us has cause to think with deep gratitude of those who have lighted the flame within us. The deepest craving of human nature is the need to be appreciated.

To begin bringing gratitude into your life, you can deliberately meditate on all the things in your own life that helps you or give you pleasure. You can also write a gratitude diary, posting pictures and writing about the things you feel grateful for each day. The holidays are a great time to express your gratitude to friends and family by writing cards and exchanging thoughtful, personal gifts.

Baking cookies for neighbors or sharing food with the poor are other ways to express appreciation for the abundance of food that we have in this country. Gratitude can lead to feelings of love, appreciation, generosity and compassion, which further open our hearts and help rewire our brains to fire in more positive ways.

People who are more grateful have higher levels of well-being. Grateful people are happier, less depressed, less stressed. Gratitude is an emotion of connectedness.

What are some of the benefits of gratitude?

Higher levels of control of their environments
Personal Growth
Purpose on life
Self-acceptance
Positive ways of coping with difficulties and challenges

Gratitude has been said to have one of the strongest links of any character trait with mental health. Numerous studies suggest that grateful people have fewer negative coping strategies.

Grateful people sleep better, because they think fewer negative and more positive thoughts just before going to sleep.

I had a friend, Ruth, who played the piano for years for her church. But she felt much unappreciated and was experiencing feelings of rejection. Eventually, with tears in her eyes, she sadly wrote a letter of her resignation to the Pastor.

"Dear Pastor Henry, it is with much regret that I am resigning my position at the Lutheran Hills Church. I want to thank you for allowing me to be of service over the last five years."

She had loved playing for the church as it was her passion, but felt invisible and that nobody cared if she was there or not.

As she walked to her mailbox to mail her resignation letter she saw that the postman already had come and there was a letter to her from someone in the church she barely knew. It was a thank you card expressing the writer's heartfelt joy in knowing that Ruth was always there filling her with hope and encouragement through her music of passion to God. Tears streamed from Ruth's eyes as she read. The heartfelt words of love that she read that day was a gift that she would never forget. She never did turn in her notice that day and as far as I know is still playing for the Lutheran Hills Church.

Show your gratitude to someone that comes to your mind every day and write down how it felt and how it affected that person. (Example: Hug, Smile, phone call, greeting card, encouraging word, gift, etc.)

When we start to count flowers
We cease to count weeds;
When we start to count blessings,
We cease to count needs
When we start to count laughter,
We cease to count tears
When we start to count memories,
We cease to count years.

"Give thanks unto the LORD; for he is good: for his mercy endured forever" (Psalms 136:1)

"Don't fret or worry. Instead of worrying, pray. Let petitions and praises shape your worries into prayers, letting God know your concerns. Before you know it, a sense of God's wholeness, everything coming together for good, will come and settle you down. It's wonderful what happens when Christ displaces worry at the center of your life." (Philippians 4:6-7)

JUST DO IT!

Taking risks in Life is better than doing nothing. Choose to take action today. Imperfect action is better than perfect inaction

As I see it. . . . . . .

1. **Decisions**– A decision sets in motion the thought process.

Take the actions needed to get the job done, at the risk that the action may not be perfect. Do the best you can with what you have from where you are.

If we wait to take the perfect action, we may never get started or act. Very seldom are any actions perfect.

Never fear to take action, when an action is needed. The following story could have been fatal for me if I had allowed fear to paralyze me. It was Christmas and I was on my way to a party. I had all the presents carefully wrapped and in the backseat of my car along with Christmas cookies, candies and pies. The music was playing Joy the World on the radio as I drove down the street. I love Christmas and I was so excited to share this special holiday with all my friends and family at the party.

As I was driving something captured my attention from below the dashboard. What was that? A flicker of something, I looked again and my heart started pounding when I looked beside me and saw fire shooting out from under the steering wheel column. In a flash of a moment I saw an image of my finger going through the flame of a candle and not being hurt, so I just knew that if I jumped with my whole body I could get the same results. I kicked off my high heel shoes and in one big push, opened the door and rolled out on to the middle of the busy street. As soon as the car slowed and landed on the side of the road, BOOM!!! The car went up in flames.

God spoke to me and showed me a picture of what I should do. I took action and my life was saved. I was saved only because I heard, took action and didn't allow fear to paralyze me.

2. Empowered – (permitting one to take ACTION)
Challenges and Thrills come when you take action. (You will either be thrilled or challenged by the action you chose, everything will unfold, the good the bad and the ugly

ACTION IS WHAT COUNTS! Take Action - When it's time to act, take action. Take the actions needed to get the job done, at the risk of the consequences of that the action. (Results of my action: no car, no presents, but I was alive and unhurt.)
If we wait to take the perfect action, we may never get started or act. Very seldom are any actions perfect

ACTION on prompting saved my life.

1. Decision is a thought.
2. Empowered (Jumping) is an Action
3. ACTION is what counts

DO IT NOW - whatever you are procrastinating to do, fearing the most, and allowing circumstances and distractions to keep you stuck and frustrated with projects. Do the things that are in your heart to do, Living your Passion and Dream

Take that leap of Action and Just Do It! We get thoughts and ideas all the time but rarely take action on those thoughts.

What Action are you taking today?

ACTION STEPS:

Activate your JOY

Laughing and finding happiness in each day and each situation that arises helps boost your body's natural immune system.

1. Spend time with people that enjoy laughing and humor
2. Smile
3. Think on things that bring you joy like children, pets, art, nature, friends, etc.

Activate your GRATITUDE

At times our own light goes out and is rekindled by a spark from another person.

1. Write a gratitude journal
2. Everyday give thanks to someone that comes to your mind like a word of encouragement, a hug, giving a gift,
3. Count your blessings every day.

What Do You See?

In the picture on the left are two possibilities. Depending on your perception you will see either a young lady or an old woman.

Chapter Eight

Gathering Evidence

I had become completely frustrated. My life at that time spoke of everything but success. It looked as though we were about to lose everything we had worked for. I didn't have a job and was staring at shut off notices from the phone and utility companies.

Worse yet, it was Christmas and it looked as though our children were going to be without presents this year. I can tell you quite honestly that I was severely depressed. Things looked absolutely hopeless, and I could see no way out. I finally convinced myself that I could at least get a cardboard sign, stand on a corner and beg for help.

I drove to the corner of Watt and Folsom and wrote out with marker on a piece of cardboard the words, NEED HELP FOR CHRISTMAS.

I'll never forget that day. As I looked out the windshield it was cloudy and drizzling rain. I sat looking out at the corner, watching the cars pass by through the rain. I felt frozen with shame, I just couldn't bring myself to get out of the van. I just sat there and sobbed.

Somehow, we made it through that crisis as well as others throughout the years. It wasn't easy, especially since I had allowed the negatives that were taking place in my life to shape beliefs about myself. I had allowed what I was experiencing to determine who I was. I looked at my world and tallied up the vote and by unanimous decision had come up short.

What had happened to me? I was creative, driven and was ready to shake my world. Yet, things had not worked out the way we had planned.

One of the dangers of past failures and defeats in our lives is that we begin to define ourselves by them. For instance, if our children struggle in school and get a failing grade, they often assume that they are dumb and stupid. If a person goes through a loss like a divorce, they may begin to believe that it must mean they are unlovable.

As humans we are very afraid about what certain events in our lives say about us as individuals. We never stop to think that maybe our study habits need some correction. We never think to ourselves that a divorce took place because of certain behaviors or expectations that were not met. We would rather decide that those painful failures are about our value and worth in this world.

Another way we sometimes deal with defeats and failures when we don't understand them is to blame God. We use words like "God is teaching me," or "God is testing me." I suppose it is easier to thrust the irresponsible acts of a world gone crazy onto God then to accept that we simply live in a world that is unpredictable and chaotic.

Country artist Bill Currington appropriately describes it in the lyrics of his song, *People Are Crazy*. He sings the words, "God is great, beer is good and people are crazy." In my book *Breaking the Cycle of Defeat*, I wrote those lyrics on the cover page.

Gathering evidence is defined as "the available body of facts or information indicating whether a belief or proposition is true or valid." By all accounts you may be looking at your situation and striking the gavel of judgment down where it concerns your life. Remember that the judgment you make about yourself is the difference between staying stuck or moving forward.

People look outside themselves for evidence, and it is on that information that they make judgments. Hey, this is a good thing if you happen to live in a perfect world where nothing ever goes wrong. Sadly though, our world doesn't work like that. We each come from a past that had its own level of dysfunction.

Viktor Frankl was a Holocaust survivor. He determined that there was one thing the Nazis could not control in his life; they could not control his attitude. He said, "The last of all human freedoms is the ability to choose one's own attitude regardless of circumstances." In other words, he couldn't control everything, but he could control himself and his attitude.

We live in a world where things deteriorate and break, a world where people live in fear and don't always do what you expect them to do. The choice is ours, pitch a tent and build our home in the rubble of our experience or refuse to define ourselves by these voices that will only keep you from moving forward.

Recognizing that I was judging myself by circumstances and refusing to be defined by my external world was a huge breakthrough moment. I remember that on many occasions I would walk through the house and affirm out loud the words, "I refuse to be defined by _____, this is not who we are as a family." When our teenagers made bad decisions, I would tell them the same thing, "This is not who you are!", and remind them who they really were.

Did everything suddenly get better? Well, things seldom change overnight. But what took place was a change within myself concerning how I saw myself and what was possible in my life.

If this is not who I am, then who am I?

When establishing the identity of a thing, you must always refer back to the manufacture as a reference point. Deciding what you believe about where you came from will establish your value in your own eyes.

If you believe that we came out of God, then our value is fixed and uncompromised. That means that you are priceless and invaluable. Based on our experience we might change our minds about our own value and contribution to our world, but God does not.

We must go back to the original blueprint and design in order to understand the intention for which it was created. What were you created for? You were created to thrive, to grow beyond the limitations and constraints that surround you. This is easy to see when looking at our world around us. Nature is in a constant state of growth because it contains within itself the genetic instruction to fulfill itself. You are no different.

This is a belief that must become an established fact within our hearts. Your surroundings do not have to define you; this is not what determines the value you have to offer your world. What you are currently dealing with in your life is only temporary!

You will either gather negative evidence or positive evidence that supports where it is you want to go in life.

Byrd Baggett, a speaker on leadership development, tells a story about his Mom, who was in the hospital. As she laid there the doctor turned to the couple and said, she will be lucky if she lives a year. Mrs. Baggett, who could barely whisper, signaled to her husband to come close so she could give him instructions. As he leaned down to his wife to hear what she had to say, she whispered, "You fire that doctor!"

Mr. Baggett walked out into the hall with that doctor and told him calmly, "You're fired." Mr. and Mrs. Baggett hired a new doctor, Dr. Thomas Runge, who loved and treated Mrs. Baggett not as a patient but as a human being. Mrs. Baggett lived not just one year, not just five or ten more years. She went on to live fifteen more years! The Baggett's attribute their miracle not only to the love and compassion of Dr. Runge but to their faith in the true healer.

What is the moral of this story? You fire the people that tell you that you can't dream big! Where can you gather good supportive evidence? There are voices all around you if you will look for them. Here are just a few resources you can reach out to.

God's view and opinion of you, which is always good! Other voices would include mentors, life coaches, supportive family members, a supportive pastor, rabbi or priest, positive books, movies, and video's, seminars, workshops, supportive online and offline communities, clubs and organizations. The list is endless, you just have to seek them out.

ACTION STEPS:

Let go of and release all previous assumptions you have accepted about your life.

When you catch yourself reaching for these old patterns, declare out loud this is not who I am.

Instead, immediately speak the opposite positive truth.

"I AM _____ "

In some cases you might consider a rubber band around your wrist that you snap whenever you are rejecting an old pattern.

After snapping, embrace the new pattern.

Chapter Nine

Turn Your Obstacles into Opportunities

Obstacles and trouble in life can be challenging, but they open up opportunities if we allow them to do so. A relentless pursuit of our dream has caused Debra and me to press through when times became tough. The end result opened doors of opportunities, many of which could be defined as miraculous.

An example of this happened many years ago. Debra and I felt inspired to move to Little Rock, Arkansas from Denver, Colorado to attend a one year Missions school that a church had started. We felt very strongly that we were to eventually end up traveling and serving as ministers in foreign countries. We had an assurance in our heart that this was the direction we should take.

Our first obstacle

Both sets of our parents thought we had lost our minds and made it their job to tell us that we were crazy, After all, we had just had our first child, who was just 4 months old.

Then the second obstacle came

We had just enough money to get there and pay for the first month's tuition and then pay for one month's rent in a mobile home. We had no promise of a job, but felt strongly about making the move.

The funny thing is that we hadn't even applied to attend the school yet. We felt that by the time we sent our application and waited for approval, classes would have already started and it would be too late. We packed everything we had into an open top U-Haul trailer and started down the road, pulling it with our green Pinto.

We must have been quite a sight when we pulled into town. It was Sunday morning and we were excited to be there. We didn't know anyone in Little Rock, so we drove straight to church that morning, parked and went in.

They had all the visitors stand up that morning and announce who they were. We proudly told the audience that we had just driven in from Denver and were there to attend Agape School of World Evangelism!

What, another obstacle?

After the service the Dean of the school signaled us and called us into his office. He told us that we should have sent in our application prior to coming and that we probably had wasted our time in making this trip. But even then we were not discouraged by what we were told, somehow we knew that everything would work out and we would be accepted.

As it turned out, we were accepted in the school and got started. A seeming miracle, but that did not solve the issue of money. Then I had an inspirational idea. I remembered having seen in Denver a successful business called the Christian Yellow Pages. Why, we could start one here and call it the Little Rock Christian Service's Directory!

Obstacle of no expertise or knowledge

Even though I had absolutely no experience, I knew that there were other students who did. I thought that perhaps this could be a great opportunity for creating an income not only for us but for other students as well. I shared it with my classmates, especially to one classmate I sat next to who had experience in the printing business.

Obstacle of no support

You probably can guess what their response was. Not one of them could see what I was so excited about. I was not to be swayed, but continued to act on the inner knowledge of the value of the idea that had come to me. I placed an ad in the newspaper and hired two people on a commission only basis. Then I had an inspirational idea to contact the two Christian Radio stations in Little Rock and traded out advertising with them. This gave me massive exposure to get my message out about the soon to be published directory! Then, I had another inspired thought! The free advertising that I had been given from the radio station could be used to leverage more sales. We were able to now give away free radio spots to Christian businesses who advertised with us. The radio spots would advertise the Christian Services Directory and then I would showcase our advertiser of the day!

We sold advertising and made money to pay for our one year stay in Little Rock Arkansas. And we were instrumental in publishing the first Christian business directory this city had ever seen. This entire endeavor was started with no out of pocket money, only an idea! We discovered that as you are moving forward on the ideas and inspirational thoughts you have, other good things will come your way as well.

As a result of acting on a prompting to make a move across the country in the midst of obstacles, we were able to build relationships with the Filipino community in Little Rock. We met these precious folks there and they volunteered to collate, sort and deliver the directory for us. They knew we wanted to go to the Philippines and they wanted to support us in our endeavor. What a Godsend!

We could have been stopped by the obstacles and quit at any time and not have experienced the many opportunities that began to come our way. An anonymous donor showed up one day at the school and paid for my entire year's tuition! One of the Filipino friends we met had a relative in Manila and that friend later hosted us during our stay in that city. Because of this relationship, we were able to pray for her sister's daughter while we stayed in their home. The daughter had been traumatized by something that had taken place in her life and as a result could not communicate. She would walk around the house in a catatonic state. This was an amazing miracle. After praying for her we were met by the parents the next morning as they thanked us over and over for what we did. She was miraculously healed and set free by the power of God.

We saw many miracles while we were in the Philippines. One time I remember, while we stayed in Manila we found ourselves out of money. We were waiting for funds to clear the bank and meanwhile had the responsibility not only of feeding ourselves but our two children and two helpers, one of whom was an intern from a Bible School.

We had run short on food that day and told everyone to stay home while we went to speak at a church across the city. We had just enough funds for transportation to our speaking engagement, but thought that perhaps the church we were visiting would take an offering for us, as other churches had done for us in the past.

After a bus, Jeepney and a tri-cycle ride to the church, and our speaking assignment, we discovered we were wrong. We left the church disheartened that night, knowing that everyone at home was waiting for dinner. We stood on the corner with barely enough money to get home. "Well, what are we going to do Debra?"

As we stood there, Debra began moving her foot on the ground as if she was trying to get something off her shoe. She reached down to remove whatever was stuck there, thinking it was wet leaves stuck to the bottom of her shoe. Instead of leaves, she discovered money! Wow, more than enough to go to the market and head home for a feast! We praised God that night for his provision in our lives. Obstacles do become opportunities when we believe that all things are indeed possible!

Over the next few years we were able to see many people impacted in many ways. The opportunities we witnessed were the result of our not allowing obstacles to stop us from moving forward. Is that to say that we have never stopped and become stuck in our thinking? No, there have been many instances in which we have allowed ourselves to give up. But when we really think about it, it was never the obstacles in our lives that stopped us, when we were thwarted it was always because we had allowed our perceptions and thinking to stop us!

It is one thing to notice the moments of inspiration in our lives and an entirely different experience to believe and act on those moments. The following statements are a few common blocks that keep us in a state of inner paralysis, preventing us from "going for it' in life:

- "I can't do that"
- "Nothing ever works out for me"
- "I can't handle rejection"
- "I am not OK if this doesn't turn out the way I want it to"
- "What will people think?"
- "What if I fail?"

Realize that it is always better to step forward into growth then to stop backward into safety.

Financial Advisor B.C. Forbes once noted that history has demonstrated that the most notable winners in history usually encountered heartbreaking obstacles before they triumphed. They finally won because they refused to become discouraged by their defeats.

ACTION STEPS:

Get use to recognizing the voice of inspiration in your life and taking some type of action quickly.

Studies show that inspired idea's and thoughts dissipate within twelve hours. Taking action simply starts with writing the it down and then asking yourself, what is the one step I can take right now?

As you have been reading this book there have been many inspired thoughts concerning new directions for your life. Have you written these new thoughts and idea's down yet?

"It still holds true that man is most uniquely human when he turns obstacles into opportunities."

~Eric Hoffer

Chapter Ten

Empowered to Live!

Being empowered means recapturing and developing your authority, esteem and initiative in your life. It is holding on to the knowledge that you have been given the authority to move forward toward your dreams, desires and ambitions. Instead of allowing your surroundings to dictate to you, you are discovering what kind of contribution you want to make to others around you and you are taking action.

People typically start out in this world with their authority intact, but it isn't very long until we begin to relinquish that authority in many ways. We know that giving up some of our personal power is necessary if we are to survive and grow in the world - We accommodate our parents, teachers and bosses - but while we are in that process we often forget our initiative concerning our own dreams and desires.

Bern Moses

As Bern sat listening to a recording that someone had given to him he wondered whether what he was hearing could help him. Another manager in the company he worked for had told him that if he wanted to move from good to great, this message would be his answer. The recording was from Earl Nightingale and was called *The Strangest Secret*.

Bern nodded to himself in agreement as Earl explained that the number one problem in our society is conformity. Millions of people go through life from day to day not thinking of themselves as being any different than the person standing next to them. These people represent 96% of our world! Over the next few days Bern pondered what he had heard on the recording.

It had been just a year or so earlier that he had started out as a sales person for the Alcoa Company. It had actually happened quite by accident. While he had been in the Navy his pay records had been lost. He was told that it would be a while until his records would be corrected. Bern had found himself in financial need and not sure what to do. It was at that time that a young man showed up at his home. He wanted to showcase a beautiful set of Cutco knives to Bern and his wife. It wasn't long after that Bern got started as a representative himself and started selling cutlery. It had seemed like his best option.

Bern's story is an amazing one. You see, Bern was an introvert and a stutterer. He had been teased and bullied about a speech impediment since he was six years old, and now he was going to talk for a living? I can still remember his voice as he introduced himself to me. "Hi, my name is Bern Mo…Moses." (By the time I had met him, you could hardly notice that he had any stutter when he talked.)

Bern never forgot those early years starting out. Facing your fears can be challenging. Bern told me that he must have fired and rehired himself at least six times on his first time out in the field. "I drove 168 city miles looking for the right house to stop at. I sat there locked up in that car literally unable to function."

Finally becoming angry with himself, he stopped the car and knocked on the door of the nearest house. As he recalls later, he was unprepared, inept and even inappropriate in his presentation but in the end, the person made a purchased. From that time forward, Bern was hooked and went on that night to sell four sets of cutlery.

Looking back on that night he admits that he never was able to replicate that event again. In fact, as he tells it, the subsequent two years were overwhelming. He would leave sales calls frustrated because he was not able to communicate what was in his heart and head. The stress at being mocked and not understood would result in him sitting in his car sobbing. As time went on, he did become good at recruiting and as a result made a few dollars in override commissions from a sales team.

Two years had now passed and Bern was thinking about leaving the Navy and going full time. The words of Earl Nightingale echoed in the back of his mind and wondered why he seemed to be stuck. He certainly hadn't made any great advances as a manager in the Alcoa job. At that time, there were approximately one thousand five hundred managers in the company and he was number one thousand two hundred plus or minus any given month. That meant there were one thousand three hundred other managers ahead of him that were doing better than he was. It also meant that after two years of work, he had only risen in the company by two hundred people.

One day while driving along, he had a flash that went through his mind that hadn't been in the recording or in a particular book he had been reading. As he describes it, it was like a psychic shift that had profound effects on him. It suddenly dawned upon him that he had been accommodating people and conditions and reacting to circumstances.

What he realized was that he never had to do that again unless he chose to do so. Rather than reacting to circumstances, he could be a circumstance …that he could become causative rather than being an effect. He could initiate rather than accommodate and he could create conditions that other people would accommodate because it is in the nature of people to do so.

As a result of the mental shift that Bern experienced that day while driving his car, good things began to happen for his business. He was able to become the number one international manager in just ninety days! During the previous ninety days nothing had changed other than a mental shift or maneuver. He represented the same product at the same price, drove the same car, and had the same wife. The only change was that he decided that he was no longer going to live according to the dictates of his environment. Instead he recaptured his authority, esteem and initiative in life.

What does this mean for your life? In what ways can you begin to take initiative in the direction of your life? Are there area's where you have been accommodating people and conditions where you can become the cause to affect change?

ACTION STEPS:

Keep in mind, the moment you make a new decision, you set into motion a new cause, effect, direction, and destination for your life.

What one decision are you making regarding the directions, attitudes and focus of your life?

Remember, a decision that is real is measured by the fact that you've taken new action.

What is that action?

The decisions you make are what will determine your destination and the eventual destiny of your life, not your conditions!

———————————

It doesn't interest me what you do for a living. I want to know what you ache for – and if you dare to dream of meeting your heart's longing. It doesn't interest me how old you are. I want to know if you will risk looking like a fool – for love – for your dreams – for the adventure of being alive.

~ Oriah Mountain Dreamer

———————————

Chapter Eleven

Five Deadly Traps That
Will Keep You Stuck

Moving forward in life is a life long journey, I don't know of anyone who woke up one day and found that they had arrived.

#1 The Trap of Having No Vision

We understand that most corporations and businesses have a vision for what it is they are trying to achieve. A corporate vision creates the guidance they need so they can stay on course and not drift from their goals. A personal vision is just as important. But, sadly, most people have never written a vision statement for themselves nor do they understand why they would even need one. The truth of the matter is that if you don't have a vision for yourself now, you can be guaranteed someone else will have one for you. Not having a direction means you will not be taking responsibility for yourself and will end up accommodating other people and conditions.

A well-known proverb says, "Where there is no vision, the people will perish." The word "perish" in the original language means to cast off restraint. This really tells us that a person who has no vision will have no direction and will be like someone wandering about in many directions.

A personal vision statement is not some futuristic wish. An example of a futuristic wish would be, "To become debt free and retire at the age of 55" or, "To be the best parent and role model to my children." Instead, answer the question "What do I want?" but state it in the present tense. Here is a definition of a vision statement:

The description of a state or a situation in which you envision yourself to be at a certain time. What do I want that can inspire others? What would attract people to decide to follow me?

You should always express it in a positive way. Example: "In 2015, I am in good shape (I don't say, I will stop smoking) and others can see it is something that makes me happy and excited."

Your vision statement starts out with "I am." Look at what you want to see in the future and put it into the present. Ask yourself the following three questions. When is it? Where is it? Who are the people around you?

Debra's vision statement is "I am joy to all I meet." My vision statement is; "I am impacting nations through media and in person, inspiring people to connect and live out their potential and purpose."

Another person's vision statement may be "I am a team facilitator of a resource network, local, regional and international."

#2 The Trap of Thinking that You No Longer Have Any Choice regarding the direction of your life

We have talked about this earlier in the book. We are in this trap when we believe that our past or present negative experiences have ultimate control over our lives. Although experience can lead us to assume this, it is, in reality, completely untrue.

Misery will try to deceive and convince you that in order to get relief something outside of yourself must first change before you will be able to change. This will keep you stuck and trapped. To change, begin to establish new beliefs that challenge this.

A man came for counseling because his wife had left him. He told the counselor that his wife told him she was leaving because he was domineering and selfish. The counselor asked if the accusation was true. He answered that it probably was.

He said that since his wife left he had not been able to go to work because he was so depressed. The counselor asked, *"Does it help?"* *"What do you mean?"* He retorted. Again the question was asked but more specifically, *"Has your choice to stay home and be depressed for these last few weeks helped you get your wife back?"* With a look of inquiry on his face the man answered, *"What do you mean my choice? You're not understanding my problem. I can't help the way I feel."*

The counselor looked back at him and responded, *"Well, it certainly is not realistic to say that staying home is going to help anything, is it?"* The man answered, *"Well, I guess not, but what else am I supposed to do?"* It was at that moment that a new understanding came to him. It told him that he did have some steps he could take, that sitting home depressed would not help his marriage.

#3 The Trap of Poor Self-worth

Having a low self-worth is partly the result of believing the previously mentioned trap. Did you know that by the age of eight, most thoughts that children have about themselves are already negative?

It seems that humans have an inherent knowledge that we are lacking something. As a result we build what I call "sandcastles" to support and reassure that we are indeed worthy. In the end, these sandcastles let us down or fall apart and our identities are shattered.

The answer to poor self-worth is to go back to the manufacturer's blueprint so you can reassess your true value. Discovering God's view and opinion of us will set us free from our own faulty analysis.

#4 The Trap of Waiting For Things to Get Better

This is a trap that many fall into at times. It is easy to fill our lives with excuses for our non-action. How convinced we are of ourselves and the reasons we concoct on why we should delay.

Zig Ziglar quoted this poem in his book years ago regarding indecision that makes a great point. It's called The Bride of White Hair (poet unknown).

The Bride, white of hair, is stooped over her cane,
Her footsteps uncertainly guiding.
While down the opposite aisle,
With a wan, toothless smile,
The bridegroom, in wheelchair, come riding.

Now who is this elderly couple thus wed?
Well you'll find when you've closely explored it,
That here is the rare
Most conservative pair
Who waited till they could afford it.

The most important thing you can do in your life is to step out and learn to take action quickly. All successful people know that it doesn't come easy and they are bound to fail more than they will succeed at anything. They are willing to learn from each failure, as it will help them make better decisions that lead to success later.

#5 The Trap of Having a Lack of Focus

Let me put it right out there. Lack of focus has a lot to do with our motivational curve. I find that if I am passionate and excited about a project it is easy for me to do what is necessary to get it done. On the other hand, I have had idea's and projects that I was excited about and allowed myself to become distracted by other things.

Asking yourself about and seeing in your mind's eye what the end result and outcome will be like can re-ignite you into action. Revisit our action steps listed in chapter four. Recognizing that we are always motivated by pleasure and move away from what is considered painful will help. Learning how to manage our psychology in this area will help keep you on track.

#6 The Trap of Negative Toxic People

We all have heard the old adage; you become who you hang around with. We tell our kids this all the time as they grow into their teen years. We often forget that this also applies to our own lives as well. Separating yourself from damaging toxins is a must if you are to move forward in your life.

Decide What Kind of Life You Really Want

What do you want your life to look like? Create the vision that resonates and gets you excited and then refuse to surrender that vision to the dictates to your surroundings and others. Get clear about your values and begin to put them on paper and how you can begin taking action steps toward them.

#1 Create a Vision Statement – You and I were meant for purpose to pursue something larger than ourselves. It is part of our DNA. Having a vision is the first step in turning the invisible into the visible. It is the foundation for all success in life. A vision statement comes out of a unique blueprint that makes each of us special. A vision statement is not future tense it instead starts with the words, "I AM", it is seeing the future in the present.

#2 Create Actionable Steps – that will assist you in realizing what it is you really want. Reach out to others around you who can support you in your endeavor. These people can be a mastermind group, coaches, experts who can guide you while you are in preparation to launch.

#3 Deployment – Take your actionable steps to the next level where you are now in launch mode. Living out and experiencing your vision. Keep in mind, imperfect action is better than perfect inaction!

ACTION STEPS:

Simply write out what this book has done for you and send it to us.
Write out some specific shifts you have made and are making in
your life. Are there new directions, choices and decisions you are
making now that you were not making before?

We love hearing back from our readers.

The footprints of our inner heart still carry within it the old patterns and mindsets of the past. Because of this we still lack the sense of ownership of that which is really ours"

~Scott Johnson – Empowered

Chapter Twelve

Transformation

What does transformation look like to you? It all starts with getting a clear mental image about what you want for your life. It is realizing that all things are possible no matter what you may be been facing! Believe that it is indeed possible to experience change in the course of your life's direction, then set the sail and begin to take action.

If you are in a place where all things seem hopeless, remind yourself, over and over if need be, that this situation or obstacle is only temporary, that it does not represent who you are or where you are going. Hope is having the vision of what is possible for your life. Faith is the engine of action that prompts you to take action.

This means that the first things you need to do is get your vision back. Your vision is a radical mind shift in how you see yourself and your future. Next, you need to support that vision with evidence that supports and confirms what it is you want.

Gathering evidence that supports your vision eventually will create inspiration, which will create motivation to take the necessary action. This is the recipe that has been used throughout many generations and that has brought about positive change.

Everyone who has ever gone on to being a positive impact in their world has had a personal struggle or obstacles which they overcame in order to transition to what they are doing today. Facing fear and challenging circumstances in your life are not easy, but they contain the seeds of your greatness. Every story of triumph I have ever heard or read proves this out.

Our biggest mistake is to look at the achievements of these people and jump to the conclusion that somehow their life was easy, they are different, that they were born lucky. More often than not, their stories came out of adversity and less than favorable circumstances.

Og Mandino

Take Og Mandino's story for instance. Og Mandino was an American author who wrote the bestselling book *The Greatest Salesman in the World*. His books have sold over 50 million copies and have been translated into over twenty-five different languages. To look at his life you would assume that success was easy for him. But on the contrary, he had been an alcoholic hobo who moved from town to town picking up what menial work he could.

Og's story was never easy, but the ultimate in degradation arrived one cheerless day in an unfriendly Cleveland, Ohio, where he contemplated putting a bullet in his skull.

Trudging through the snow, Og found himself outside a public library and went in to keep warm. Wandering amongst the many bookshelves he found himself staring at the section headed "Self-help, Success and Motivation." This became the tipping point in his life and was the first of many visits to various public libraries.

I believe that there is a voice that calls out to each of us and tells us, if we will listen, that we can indeed rise above our obstacles. Sadly, many choose to listen to other voices that tell them that they can't. Og Mandino came face to face with the voice of hope that day in the library and chose to take action.

Marilyn Van Derbur

Marilyn Van Derbur's story is an amazing one. By all accounts she was a successful woman, having been crowned Miss America while attending the University of Colorado. After receiving a Bachelor of Arts degree she chose to become a public speaker as a career. Since her career began, Marilyn has received numerous awards and acknowledgments for her work, including being the first woman to be given the highest speaking award possible by the National Speakers Association and induction into the Colorado Women's Hall of Fame.

Marilyn explains that at the age of forty-five to age fifty-one her life completely shut down. She would find herself lying on the floor sobbing with vivid memories and feelings came back to her of incest by her father from age five to age eighteen. She was hospitalized, locked in a psychiatric ward with complete paralysis of her arms and legs. To her it was a dark secret to never be shared, that is until the Denver Post broke the story. Marilyn just knew that from that moment on her career would be over. The utter shame that she felt had convinced her that all the respect and success that she had built would be over. A press conference followed, and again both major papers ran front page stories. Soon after, one of Marilyn's sisters went public as well about her own experience.

The turning point happened a few days later when Marilyn was stopped by a woman who wanted to talk. She told Marilyn that it was a good thing that her sister had gone public because now that she had, people did not believe that this could have happened would now believe. Marilyn was stunned; she turned to the woman and asked, "If people will not believe a fifty-three-year-old me, then who is going to believe a child?" That became the turning point of her life and career. From that moment forward, Marilyn went on and turned her focus from her own pain to the pain of incest others were suffering from. She has devoted much of her adult life to raising national awareness and understanding of sexual abuse and its long-term effects. In 1989 her family funded an adult incest survivor program in Denver, and in 1993 she co-founded two national not-for-profit organizations dedicated to public education and strengthening laws protecting victims of sexual abuse.

For her tireless work in the area of childhood sexual trauma awareness Marilyn has received many awards and much recognition, including the "Exceptional Achievement in Public Service from the Secretary of Health and Human Services, Washington D.C.". Since her story of incest became public, Marilyn has spoken in over 500 cities and answered tens of thousands of letters and emails from survivors looking to her for support.

Marilyn has turned her pain into a way she can make a difference in the lives of others.

Take for instance the following modern day stories from just a few people we know in our personal lives.

Gail Hamilton

Gail Louise Hamilton was born two and a half months premature. The 100% oxygen which was placed into her incubator 24/7 for the first six weeks of Gail's life left her with partial sight. Raised in an abusive, unsupportive family, one of isolation and negativity, not much hope was given to Gail that she would ever live a normal life, much less a life filled with success.

It was her Grandma's love that guided Gail through life's many challenges and obstacles, one of which was having become totally blind at eleven years of age. In spite all of this, Gail was able to achieve a Bachelor of Arts degree, a Master of Music degree with emphasis in vocal, a Master of Arts degree in Psychology and Counseling and even helped build her own Habitat for Humanity House. Her dream of singing and speaking publicly has become a reality.

In June of 2013, Gail won the title of Ms. Colorado Senior America and represented Colorado at the National Ms. Senior America pageant finals in Atlantic City, New Jersey in October.

Gail was the first blind woman ever to enter and be awarded 4th runner up in this competition! This has given Gail the platform to widen her opportunities to speak and perform and spread her message of living a life of greatness. She believes that in order to fulfill our dreams we need to find our passion, be creative, follow our hearts and trust in God.

Vision to Gail is internal, not external, and is guided by her heart and not her eyes.

LeAnn Thieman

An "ordinary person," LeAnn Thieman struggled through extraordinary circumstances and found the courage to succeed. As a 25-year-old nurse and mother she faced her fears and took a step of faith. In 1975 LeAnn helped raise money and supplies for the war orphans of Viet Nam. In April she agreed to escort 6 babies from Saigon to their adoptive homes in the USA. By the time she arrived in Vietnam, bombs were dropping outside the city! She was greeted with, *"Have you heard the news? President Ford has okayed 'Operation Babylift'. You'll help take out not 6, but 300 babies!"*

Her powerful story of rescuing the babies to be brought to the U.S. as Saigon was falling to the Communists has molded her path as a nurse speaker and author of 12 "Chicken Soup for the Soul" books. Believing we all have individual "war zones," she now inspires people to balance their lives, truly live their priorities and make a difference in the world.

What will your transformational story look like?

Realize that in every obstacle, frustration, difficulty and fear you face there lies within it the hidden the seeds of greatness. Ask any great person of achievement and they will tell you that there is no lack of opportunity in the world. Why you may ask? Because opportunities were once obstacles and we know there is never a shortage of those.

Debra and I believe that life does not have to end with regret or failure. We believe in the power of hope that the power to lift you up and make you soar. Hope is tireless in its voice and constantly speaking to you that "All things are possible to them who believe." Resolving to move forward no matter the circumstance, and yes, failing again and again is far better than doing nothing.

ACTION STEPS:

Describe what you see for yourself in the most positive way possible. Creating a compelling vision for yourself that will motivate you and keep you in the game is important. It goes back to what we refer to in our first chapter in setting the sail of your life.

Create an image that is so strong that it excites you. Again write down all the benefits and positive outcomes of you taking action. As you create this compelling vision, pay attention to the inspired ideas that come to you and learn to take action quickly.

"Courage and initiative come when you understand your purpose in life."

~ John C. Maxwell

In Closing

Nothing gives us as much joy as hearing the words, "You changed my life." It is our passion to see you experience results in your life. We believe that you have genius on the inside of you, a world of possibility that lays in quite solace waiting to be awakened.

Our belief is that every human on this planet has a voice that should be understood, explored and lived. Once you understand and have discovered your own sound in the world, it is to be lived out with passion and purpose. Grant it, your own definition of how that looks and sounds, is unique only to you and now must be deployed.

Your obstacles and setbacks are a part of the grand orchestra that will resonate with those that need to hear your voice. As you accept this new position, your transformation becomes complete.

As you're sharing your gift to the world you are completing the cycle of healing and transformation that our world is in desperate need of.

As we finish this book together, we hope it is the start of your journey, from wherever you happen to be now in your life toward the fullest most complete expression possible.

We also hope that this is the start of our journey together. If you have a desire to continue on to the next step and be a part of one of our programs be sure to join our network at our website at: www.GraceEmpoweredLiving.com

Visit our page and find out about our new workshop and program

**How To Discover, Develop, Deploy Your
Unique Brand and Voice In The World**

*Find Your Voice
Live You're Passion
Touch Your World*

Made in the USA
San Bernardino, CA
14 April 2015